The Covering Of God

Lennell Haley

Published in Oklahoma by:
Lennell Haley, KIRM INC Ministries
City of Tulsa, Oklahoma

Typography by:
Deidra Tutt Jackson, Jade Business Resources
        jadebr@live.com
Sherrie Wallace

Edited, proofed, and prepared for publishing by:
Deidra Tutt Jackson, Jade Business Resources
        jadebr@live.com

Photography:
Book Cover courtesy of:
C.King Photography, Luray, VA
        c.kingproductions@gmail.com
https://www.facebook.com/charleskingphotography

DEDICATION

To LeRoy Haley, Jr., who at age 56 years young
was diagnosed with dementia

*I will lift up mine eyes to the hills from whence
cometh my help, my help cometh from the Lord,
which made heaven and earth.*
Psalm 121:1-2

i

Dementia

Quietly I spoke as my voice began to fade away. My body began taking on a new form while my brain told me to say and do things that were unkind to myself and others.

I often laughed thinking that I still have it going on, calling my loved ones by other names and looking at their faces as though I was meeting them for the first time.

Tumbling all the way back to my very beginnings of time, remembering only those who had passed away, yes, we all chat with one another from time to time.

But you know what? Dementia is like a dream that I can't wake up from. It doesn't hurt because like I said, I think I still have it going on.

I am so sorry to hurt all the ones I love, like my daughter, Lakiesha, and my grand-daughter, Keyshawna.

NeNe always tells me that I have a wife, but I'm sorry I don't remember you (Delores) and I know that must have hurt.

I can call my sister's names Shariel and Sandra and brother Darryl. But if you were standing here in front of me, I would make you sad because I wouldn't remember your faces.

To my mother, Jonell, and my daddy, LeRoy, I do remember your voices... thank goodness.

As for Ne Ne, that's what I call my oldest sister, Lennell, you are taking good care of me. Everyone should not be mad at you. I told you when I was able to speak and make decisions for myself, that I wanted and chose to be with you.

I LOVE YOU GUYS

LeRoy Haley Jr.

P.S. My prayers are that I will walk out of the hospital well and not remember any of this, so, just know that God is not through with me yet.

-Rev. Lennell Haley

Be Blessed
Isaiah 53:5; 1 Peter 2:24 and 2 Kings 20

Contents

A Poem for a Poetess, by Charell Williams

What do you dream of as you sleep?
Did you know the moon is at 98%?
Who knows where all the time went?

Rivers flow, east and west.
Sometimes separating,
and again, being next to each other,
again and again.
Sometimes, I can now take,
Sometimes, out the last line.
Do poets rhyme line by line?

Maybe poets talk real stuff like this,
but end up getting hooked like a fish.
As a 30-year-old son,
who made it out the hood,
Yes, you did, Yes, I did, Yes, we did, and
Yes, we can.

Wisdom is infinite, you have proven that,
as we all travel to that undiscovered country,
whose born no traveler returns.

Your son is now a traveling man.
Now who knows
what is the right hand to extend?
You may never understand.
You may understand fully.
Thank God for him, not being a bully.

Seek Wisdom is what I say.
I remember now, you said that everyday

A poem for a poet, from a poet's son.
At last the journey to our destiny, has begun

Godspeed Mother
The Poet's Son
February 10, 2009; 10:58 p.m

Negative

I remember sitting down one day,
surrendering my negative thoughts
over to the Most High.

The Holy Spirit steps in
taking charge with a piece of paper
and pen at hand.

He began giving me words to jot down.
Some would rhyme from time to time.

I started paying close attention,
as I began realizing
that the Lord was using
a broken down person like me
to spread a word or two
about my life and others,
turning negative thinking
to something beautiful.

Out of the blue I began noticing the blue skies
and the sprinkling stars shining bright.
Telling me and so many others:

To trust and believe
that all things work together
for those who love the Lord.

Romans 8:28

Jazmine, Mateo and Brennell

To my three wonderful grandchildren,
I want each of you to know
that I ask the Lord each night
to tip-toe into your bedrooms
and give each of you a kiss on your foreheads.

Then I ask the Lord
to leave a little note in your hearts
letting you know that
that kiss was from Grandma.

I love you very much.

A Hard Lesson Learned Through Stupidity

Just taking an innocent walk today,
I learned a life lesson the hard way.
No matter how you look at it,
there is no excuse for stupidity.

Sometimes my stupidity
shows up unexpectedly,
which causes pain to myself.
Now you can see,
I am not as smart as you think I am.

I can sometimes look the part of being smart,
when really I am not.
And if you don't believe me,
just stick around for a few minutes
and my stupidity will show up.

Stupid people can't keep asking
the smart ones to forgive them
each time they make a stupid mistake.
Somewhere smart people must draw the line
when they come in contact with people like me
from time to time.

We don't mean any harm,
we are just stupid people you see,
who sometimes get in our own way
saying things we need not say.

Once again I ask for your forgiveness
for the pain and discomfort
that I cause upon you today
due to one of my stupid moments
that came up at the wrong time today
while doing our walk.

I guess we never know
where we are going to be from time to time
when there is a hard lesson learned
through stupidity.

Hebrews 3:8

Rosebud

I am writing this little note
to a very special young lady
whom I have had the opportunity
to see grow from a wildflower
to a beautiful rosebud.

Understanding now
that the beauty she holds
comes from God above
as she continues down life's path.

I want her to remember
to hold onto her rosebud
because it represents
the unconditional love
that Jesus Christ has for her
on this special day
and always.

Okay, Rosebud.

2 Corinthians 11:2

If I Could Give You A...

Red Rose
For the way you live your life
in front of me.

White Rose
For the unconditional love
that you share with me.

Pink Rose
For the wonderful things
you have taught me.

Purple Rose
For your royalty.

Blue Rose
For your gracefulness.

But
Since some of these colored roses
don't exist---
Please close your eyes
while I whisper something sweet
in your ear

Happy Mother's Day

To You

Shattered Dreams Have No Color

Poetry is sometimes recognized
as freedom of speech,
expressing one's point of view.
Sometimes the words will rhyme,
and sometimes they won't.
I would like to try, without offending anyone.
I often think about the wonderful speech
that Martin Luther King Jr. gave
in the early sixties,
when I was just a little girl.
The speech was called;

"I Have A Dream"

Seems like everyone understood the dream
except for us.

Without playing the race card
what happened to us?
Where is the natural beauty we used to have?
What happened to all the businesses
our mothers and fathers used to own?
We wasn't the only ones in both race riots.
What happened to our children
listening to us?
What happened to our men respecting us,
and us respecting them?
Our mothers loving and taking care of us,
no matter what?

What happened
to all the hard work we used to do
just to make our ends meet?

Tell me what happened to our freedom
to make positive choices?
What happened to our children's laughter?
What happened to us supporting one another?

The Lord made a promise to us,
that He will not allow our dreams to die.
That's why He blessed us with
a new President for the next 4 years,
giving every citizen of the United States;

Opportunities–Being–Accepted–Making–Amends

Acts 2:17-21

Finally

I finally allowed myself
to leave the past behind me.

Learning to love myself unselfishly;

I do not consume negativity,
gossiping or judging others
in my life today.

I relax, breathe,
and enjoy life to the fullest today,
the way the Lord desired me to.

Try living right today,
and begin to enjoy all that life has to offer you.

Deuteronomy 6:2

God

With God's faith,
He created a universe.
Then He decided to have a Son
who will rule the heavens and earth
and everything in them.

Wanting someone to walk
through His promised land
with His blood,
He created each one of us.

All the different nationalities and languages
come from God above.
We had nothing to do with
the color of our skin.

His dream is for each one of us
to return back home to Him,
clapping and praising Him
in Jesus Christ's name,
Amen!

Genesis 1:1

Don't Hate

I just found out the other day,
that my ex-husband passed away.

How quickly my heart turned cold as ice,
once again,
I have no wonderful memories of him.

The Lord spoke telling me,
"Don't Hate",
He even said He will coach me along the way,
knowing that my ex can't hurt me anymore.

Drinking, getting drunk,
causing confusion in our home.
And yet, I loved him very much once.
A mental abuser he was.

I allowed this man to take all my personality
and dignity away from me,
just to keep peace in our home.
As hard as it was,
the Lord said to me,
"Don't Hate" him.

I had to come out of my mortal body
into the marvelous light of Jesus Christ
just to find a kind word to say about him.

Only because I once loved him very much,
and love carries no fear or hate.

1 John 4:18

Little Ol'e Man

Today I met a young man
about the age of 102 years old.

As his hands began to wiggle
trying to pull his change out,
he began thinking and trying
to tell us about the good old days
and the things he used to do.

I noticed his eyes was carrying
a lot of history around
from all the places he has been.

Never having the chance to meet
my real grandpa,
just that fast, I adopted him.

Wishing he was a little younger and stronger,
I was visualizing myself sitting
on my grandpa's lap
as he shared his history
of all the places he has been.

Our elders have so much to share with us
that can help us through.
If only we would give them
a few minutes of our time to listen to them.
They been where we are trying to go.
Think about it...
be a blessing,   visit an elder today.

Psalm 71:15-18

My Better Half

I thank God each day
for allowing you to pass my way.
Becoming best friends,
we take each other's hand in marriage.

You my love, you are a silhouette of me.
It's funny,
how you sometimes complete my sentences
knowing some of my thoughts,
being strong when I am a little weak,
even cheering me on from time to time.

Baby, when I look your way
please don't turn away from me
because when I look at you
I see the better half of me.

Ephesians 4:32

Music

I hear the music as the waves wash ashore,
as the birds sing by my window pane.
Listening to the rocks
as they began tumbling down.

While the wind blows through the trees,
and the sand on the ground,
listening to someone as they
tap, tap on the drums.

Now someone stands up
blowing the horn,
while listening to someone playing
those beautiful piano notes.

Now someone is bold enough
to step to the mic
letting their pretty voice be heard.

Ephesians 5:19

Storm

The worst storms are taking place
all over the world,
making history,
from state to state.

Water is everywhere,
no heat,
food,
lights.
Phone services are shut down,
children and babies are crying.

But

Through it all,
the Christian folks must have faith.
Knowing that God is in full control.
Knowing everything will be okay.

Romans 6:19

Complaining

This has been a year for complaining,
not being appreciative
for the blessings we do have.

Like the three little bears,
trying to settle in,
nothing is right for us.

We need to learn
to appreciate what we do have
and that's life.

Today start learning how to live it.
And be content.

Philippians 2:14

Break In

Before I left my home the other day
I anointed it
and pleaded the blood of Jesus over it.

Satan decided
to send a few of his best friends in my home,
trying to destroy my peace and happiness.

What he meant for bad
Jesus will step in and turn it all around.
Satan's friends
will begin to speak in an unknown tongue.

Praising and calling out
to a new best friend,
not knowing the things they touched
and the things they took from my home
were anointed in Jesus Name.

The Lord has a way
of spreading the Good News about who He is.

Just goes to show you,
God doesn't just work through holy folks,
He also works through the least of them.

So before you think so highly of yourself,
or want to do evil toward someone else,
make sure they are not one of
God's anointed ones.

Psalm 27:1-6

A Little Boy in a Man's Place

Why do lonely mothers tell their young sons
that they are the head of the family home?

Then when a so-called new man comes along
the son begins wondering where he belongs.
What happened to the son
that was the head of the home?

Now she wants to tell her son
it's time for him to leave,
get out and get his own.

I am so sorry, son,
for making such a big mistake on my lonely days,
making you the head of the home.

It's not right for me to put you through that
knowing you are too young.
Putting a little boy in a man's place.
Leaving you to wonder
just where do you belong.

1 Corinthians 13:11

H.I.V.

I don't look down on anyone
who says they're infected with H.I.V.

Lying in a supposed-to-be-safe hospital bed
as the life of red drips in their vein.

Young people and some old schools
give their bodies away
just because someone is cute or cool.
Now that three-letter word is killing folks.

In the mother land women are being raped.
Most of their babies are being born
with no place, voice or hope.

Lord, I wonder what does the future hold
for us now that so many are infected
with that sad word called H.I.V.

Dear Lord, Lay Your Hand Upon This Nation,
In Jesus precious name,
Amen

Romans 13:13

Y Me Mother

You asked God and He gave you a daughter, but
all your men comes before me.
You even got the nerve
to cook and wait on them.
When was the last time
you invited me to dinner?

Y Me Mother,
You asked God and He gave you a daughter, yet
you have no positive words to share with me,
but then again you never do.
Always judging and comparing me to others...

Y Me Mother,
You asked God and He gave you a daughter...
All the material things
you buy most of the time,
I don't ask or want them
but you buy them anyway
and it's not for me,
it's so you can brag to your so-called friends.

Y Me Mother,
You asked God and He gave you a daughter...
You gave me a name at birth but how often
does that nasty name that people refer to
as a pregnant dog do you call me?

Y Me mother,
You asked God and He gave you a daughter...
Why did you have me? What?
You needed someone to take your abuse?
What have I done to you
for you to hate me like you do?

Y Me Mother,
You ask God and He gave you a daughter...
...I know the Lord doesn't make mistakes,
but sometimes I find myself asking Him,
Why did He have to take my daddy
away from me so soon?

Y Me Mother,
You asked God and He gave you a daughter...
If my dad was still here with me,
I know that
I wouldn't have to take your abuse.
My dear godmother tries to instill positive
words in me when you let her see me,
but you hate her too.

Y Me Mother,
You asked God and He gave you a daughter...
But that's okay too
because soon I will be able to leave you.
I am not going to say I hate you mother,
because it would be so easy for me to do.

Y Me Mother,
You asked God and He gave you a daughter...
Instead I am going to pray to God
that He will release you out of your hellhole
and also ask for prayer that I will stop hating
myself because I can't hate you.

Y Me Mother,

You asked God and He gave you a daughter..

I look into the clouds and ask,

is this a dream,

and the Lord said, "No,"
it's an answer to a prayer,

you are My Child,

Daughter

Proverbs 29:15

Don't Rush

I don't know about the rest of you
but I am not in a rush to get to heaven.

Let me tell you why!
I just realize that Jesus Christ
is right here on earth with me.
Everywhere I go, He's there.

He is about living,
that's why He walked away from the tomb.
And just like my heavenly brother,
I have so many things left yet to do
and so many things yet to come.

Heck, I still have a lot of living to do.

I understand that God is the only one
who knows the time and date
when my body will become weary
and ready to go home to be with Him.

When I get there,
Lord knows
the only thing I would like to hear is
Jesus Christ telling the Father
how wonderful I lived.

Matthew 22:32

Physical Hell

Physically speaking,
I just came from hell.
Trying to live, comfort, and be caring and
understanding around my family members.

That was the worst thing
I could have ever done.

I've come to the conclusion
that my family will never be like
one of those TV family shows.

Never do I want to physically visit hell again.
I made a choice to kiss each one of them on
the forehead and I walked away
in the still of the night,
knowing that I would not see them again soon.

I have grown
and I am okay for now with this
because it comes a time
when we must let things go.

That hurts us and it's not fair for either party.

I do wish each one of them well
and pray that they all will be all right.

Here is a toast to all of you.

Matthew 5:21-22

My Aunt's Laughter

My aunt's laughter
was full of mercy and grace
that followed her all the days of her life.
She was ninety-one years old, full of wisdom
and didn't mind sharing it
with anyone who would listen.

Oh!
What a wonderful celebration
that is about to take place.
The time has come for my aunt's laughter
to take a sweet rest.
The Lord blessed my aunt's laughter
with a beautiful sunset that she always loved.

Wow so many beautiful angels around her bed
getting her prepared for the flight of her life.
Look at her
sharing her laughter one more time
while putting her new glorious angel wings on.

Right now I bet she is trying to make sure
that there is nothing left undone.

That's my auntie, always saying,
"hold on someone is at the door",
and this time to her surprise it's Jesus Christ.

Asking my aunt Rosie Powell
if He could come in.
Asking her was she ready to go.

December 12, 2008

This day I set aside for your special celebration
to come home with Me.

John 14:2

Comforter

Oh how it hurts.
I really thought that
I would be able to handle this.
My mother is gone home to be with the Lord.
I know that one day we all must go that way.

Lord, thanks for sending someone my way
in my time of need.
I felt so all alone
but now I have a comforter
that I know speaks and works through You.

For the last three days
so many tears have I shed
trying to find answers.
How do I tell my son
that his other grandma is gone?
One that he will never know.

But
I thank God each night for allowing my son
to have another nana and his two grandpas
who love him very much
and will help me to teach and care for him.

Lord, please don't let me
leave out my son's dad
who loves and cares for him
each and every day.
Thanks for picking him to be my son's dad.

Dear Lord, I already know
you're going to take good care
of my mom, right?

Understanding the Word

As I read the Lord's words underlined in red
it says to love my neighbors as myself
and keep my heart pure.

So many holy folks always trying
to tell someone they're not living right.
Lord, I find myself sometimes
not being able to breathe.

Father, Your words tell me
now that I have been born again in You
that I can enjoy my life, decent and in order,
keeping everything in balance.

You never told me that I had to stop playing
dominoes, playing pool, listening to music,
dancing laughing or
having a glass of red wine.

Lord, tell me, am I thinking wrong
as a child of the Most High?

Lord, I want to say thank You for allowing me
to learn to listen to You and
understand Your word.
Being an example of how I am to live
and enjoy life
each day in perfect balance

Ephesians 5:6

That's My Mother

That's my mother
the lady who was standing there beside you
as we all witnessed the both of you
repeating your vows before God.

That's my mother
the lady that we all saw love you each day
unconditionally no matter what
you brought her way.

That's my mother
the one you choose to mentally abuse
not loving her the way she was loving you.

That's my mother
the one who hid it all away
putting on a front
around both our family members.
Now you have the nerve to blame her
for what you are taking her through.
This didn't just happen out the blue.

That's my mother
you must realize what you have done to her
will come back to haunt you.

That's my mother
knowing if she makes the first step
the Lord will see her through
her hurt and pain giving her the strength
to walk away from you
back into the marvelous light of Him.

That's my mother
who understands that love
does hide a multitude of faults
and it hurts when you love someone
then you find out
that they really didn't love you.

1 Peter 3:7

A True Friend

A true friend
is not someone
who has to be in your face all the time.

A true friend
is there for you in the midst of hard times,
cheering you on when things get a little rough,
while going through the storms of life.

A true friend
is always there to help you
celebrate the good times
and sharing positive words just because.

And if we have the opportunity
to meet just one true friend
then know for sure
that is a blessing from God above.

Proverbs 17:17

Fell From Grace

Going to church, reading her Bible every day,
working hard, taking care of her children,
a very pretty lady she once was.

She lost her way
when she gave her soul away.
God being a jealous God took everything
away from her except for her so-called man
that she always put first.

A saint who fell from grace.
Losing her way from the tears of life.
Allowing Satan to come,
teaching her how to lie, steal and how
to slowly kill herself smoking dope and
so many other wrong things
she has begun to do.

Now she looks like the world does.
Jesus Christ allowed her to continue
to run wild, filling up on a lot of hardship
and pain for a while
as things began to get worst
on her so-called end.

Somewhere she began recognizing and
remembering that she was a saint
who just fell down
but can get up again if she chose to.

She began apologizing
for putting everything before God.
Crying out loud she began asking
the Lord to forgive her of all her sins.
Which He did.

Then Jesus Christ
took her by the hand telling her
it's time to come home with Him.

Ephesians 5:6-17

Until Death Do Us Part

Be ye ready at all times
because we never know
from one second to the next
when God will be calling us home.

Oh
What a way to go.
I couldn't scream,
because I had no voice.
I couldn't run, because I was bed ridden.
I was trying to make some kind of sound
for my dear husband to hear me.

As I lay there, I began thinking to myself,
what a lonely way to go,
as the smoke began to fill up our home.

Just as I was giving up,
my husband found his way to me.
I begged the Lord
to get my husband out of there,
but instead,
my husband began repeating his vows
that he had made to me.
Saying for better or worse,
for richer or poorer,
in good times and in bad times,
until death do us part my dear.

He caught my hand,
holding onto it as tight as he could,
as he began calling out
in Jesus Christ's Name.

The Lord heard his cry,
then He caught us both by the hand
and took us home
to be with Him.
Yes, our Lord,
Jesus Christ

Ephesians 5:22-25

The First Day

On the first day that I met you,
I sensed you were a Christian just like me.

Sometimes we get a little discouraged,
but we must always remember,
even when we are feeling a little overwhelmed,
we must start thinking about
what God has already brought us through.

Do you know why?

Because He is the same to you today
as He was to you on the first day
that you met Him.

Now pick yourself up
and begin to praise Him
like you never have before.

Start thanking Him for another day,
allowing His Spirit to flow through you.

In Jesus name

Amen

Life's War Zone

People running all over the place.
here in my neighborhood.
Putting up security window guards,
while locking themselves in
with security screens.

I'm sitting here looking at everything
that is going on around me.
Gang-bangers
taking over the old neighborhood,
claiming streets they don't pay taxes on.

Tagging buildings,
while making empty houses their new homes.
Shooting off guns,
trying to make people scared,
while calling out their hood name.

Bad attitudes,
no sense of direction in their lives.
We're all acting just like them,
like we don't know who Jesus Christ is.

I caught myself saying,
Lord what am I going to do
to protect my family?
No funds to run out buying this or that.
So tell me Lord, how do I protect my family?

Jesus Christ just simply replied,

My child it's simple.
Get your anointing oil,
Go outside and anoint around your windows
and all your doors then go back inside.

I want you and your family to pray,
asking Me to forgive you of all your sins.
Then I want each one of you
to take communion in My Name.

Believing what you have prayed for,
start dancing and praising Me
in spirit and in truth
until I tell you to come back out again,
when everything is through.

Matthew 6:27

Sweet Tunes

I close my eyes to the universe,
as I wander off for a little while.

Then I return back feeling renewed.

Listening to the birds as they hum
a sweet tune.

Romans 12:2

Pity Party

It's time for us to shine –
come out that hell hole
that we have allowed our negative thinking
to put us in.

Pity parties take us down
to places we have never dreamed of.

We can have anything that our heart desires
if it lines up with the word of God.

But only we can change our way of thinking
and don't let anyone tell us
that it can't be done.

We must get out of our pity party bed,
get off the sofa of our comfort zone,
and then out the kitchen,
where we know we don't belong.

We must walk away in faith,
even if our faith right now
is the size of a mustard seed.

Let's do something different today.
Allowing the Lord to show us a new way
of doing positive things with our thinking.

We must remember to pray first,
then have a little faith
knowing and understanding
that without works on our part
nothing is going to take place.

No one owes us anything.
Yes, it's already in us
if we would allow ourselves a chance.

Right now let's take out a piece of paper
and write down everything that we are thinking
beginning with our dreams,
and how we can make them come true.

Pity parties take us to hell, and guess what?
We will not find Jesus Christ there.

Psalm 40:17

No One Cares

I'm not at home anymore.
I go to bed now with no cover
or blanket to cover up.

They throw two pieces of bread at me and say,
here, you can make a sandwich,
and told me,
I bet not think about asking
for a piece of lunch meat.

No One Cares.

I don't even get my own clothes anymore.
Nothing fits me.
My clothes
coming out a second-hand garbage bags.

Empty pockets, broken-down dreams.
I even quit looking for hope for tomorrow.
A little foster child I am now.
As someone makes a choice
to take me away from my home.
I have no voice about anything.
I just have to act like everything is okay.

I'm praying that tonight
as the Lord hears my prayer
He will bless a kid like me,
knowing no one cares.

Mark 10:15-16

Big Momma

Sitting here on the park bench
looking at my grandchildren
playing having fun.

How time has passed watching them.
While laughing out loud to myself,
thinking this is what Big Momma used to do.

Sitting here on this same park bench,
wondering if she could still slide or swing.

Big Momma and I used to talk
about the good old days.

Now I understand why

As I began to watch and wonder the same.

Hebrews 10:25

Renewing My Mind

I must understand
that people will always have something to say
about me whether it's positive or negative.

Today,
if someone wants to speak something negative,
I will not get upset,

Because today, I am renewing my mind.

If someone comes to help me,
showing me the right way of doing things,
because for years, I have been doing it wrong,
I will allow myself to accept positive feedback.

Because today, I am renewing my mind.

Oh what a wonderful day.
Knowing I am highly favored
by my Lord and Savior
Jesus Christ.

Because today, I am allowing my mind
to be renewed in Him,
Jesus Christ.

Hebrews 11:16

Little Brown Squirrels

Invited me to have lunch with them today
while they were running up and down the tree
eating all the fruit they saw.

I was sitting there on my balcony
enjoying a baked piece of fish
and green salad, you see.

And

If I didn't know any better,
I think those little brown squirrels
were having a conversation with me.

I began wondering
what they could possibly be saying.

Who in their wildest of dreams,
knowing at the right time,
that I would get invited to lunch
by a few little brown squirrels
sitting there looking at me,
as I looked back at them,
while we were enjoying a wonderful
lunch together.

The Beauty of Life

The beauty of life
is the breath that God grants us to take
every second of the day.

In the springtime,
when everything is so wonderful and green,
being able to see life all around us.

Knowing that we have the power
to change things
from wrong to right
just by learning
to walk in faith and not by sight.

Today I will share
only a few teardrops of sadness
and then return to a life full of laughter.

Seeing all of God's beautiful creations
that were left behind for me to enjoy.

Then knowing also,
if I am a child of the Most High,
I can ask Him to forgive me
of all my adversities.

And without a doubt,
knowing that He hears me
and it's a done deal.
So what is it that I have to complain about,
now that I understand the beauty of life?

Acts 17:27-28

Serpent

A serpent crawled across my front door today,
but the Lord was right there
to see how much I have grown in Him.

Jesus reminded me that there was no need to
panic because I belong to Him, right?

He said Satan can't do anything to you
if you don't allow him to.

I just would like to see how a child of Mine
is going to react to the unexpected.

Well I stood boldly,
saying out loud in the name of Jesus Christ,
"no weapon formed against me will prosper
in Jesus Christ's name
Amen".

I told that serpent,
"you will not disturb my peace,
so get out from around here
because you have no place here".

I am a child of the Most High.
So I closed my front door,
and that night I said my prayers,
and didn't worry about anything.

I went to bed and went right to sleep.

Psalm 56

Trusting

I know who I am today.

A child of the Most High.

In this house,
I will serve the Lord all the days of my life.

After I prayed my nighttime prayer,
I closed my eyes and went to sleep.

None did I worry through the night
because I trusted the Lord completely,
with all that I have,
and that's me.

Psalm 32:10

My Mother's Womb

For the next nine months,
off to school my embryo must go.
Still too early to tell whether I am a boy or girl,
but guess what,
right now, God knows which one I am.

My brain is fast at work,
and my tiny little heart
is beginning to do its thing.

Physics is a very important subject for me
right now because
it's going to carry me through
my nine months of schooling.

Surprisingly, I won't be able to share
any of the unknown because
I will not remember it once I am born.

Sounds of the ocean I hear in my ears.
Now all of a sudden,
I hear someone calling me
saying come out please.

I'm thinking to myself,
why would I want to leave my comfort zone
just to start all over again?

Luke 1:42

That Girl from L.A.

I am a girl who resides in L.A.
Yes, it's a pretty big city.
So many things I could get into,
good or bad and even in between.

There goes my mind taking over.
Trying to be the boss.
Wanting me to say yes,
but my humble spirit says no way.

I used to see so many negative things around.
Never seeing the other side of other people
that may be going off to work,
to make an honest living for today.

So many
dope dealers, gang-bangers, hood rats,
want-to-be crazy folks all over the place.
And homeless people everywhere.
If you can name it then more than likely
L.A. can easily claim it with no doubt.

Oh, but when I got saved,
I started hearing my name
being called from among them.
Seemed like everything about me
began to change.

Now all I can see
is positive and good things in others.

People are saying I have changed.
I used to say no, I am still the same
because all I could see in myself
was still the girl who lives in L.A.

Hebrews 11:1

A Man of Courage

Dear man of courage,
through it all you stayed.

Helping to raise, love and teach our children.
Many nights I watched you
as you sat in the rocking chair
putting them one by one to sleep.

And when they weren't feeling well
you would lie right there by their side,
rubbing their forehead back and forth,
assuring them that they would feel all right.

When it was my turn to go to work,
you stayed there trying to cook and feed them.

So today, I would like to say to you,
a man of courage,
thanks so much, for sticking around,
loving your children unconditionally too.

1 Corinthians 16:13

Waiting

Sitting here waiting,
while life is passing me by.

Waiting for two special phone calls.

You see, I have two grown children
who mean the world to me.

Day One passes,
the phone don't ring.

Day Two,
I give them both an excuse.

Day Three,
I tell a lie to myself.

Day Four,
I'm having a pity party,
feeling sorry for myself.

Day Five,
I'm still waiting for the phone to ring.

Day Six,
Yes, I am still waiting,
but now laughing to myself.

Day Seven,
Realizing it's time for me
to make a life for myself.

Ephesians 5:15-20

Thinking Like an Elephant

A elephant is huge and strong and smart,
because it never forgets anything.

They do have a weak spot for their trainers,
allowing them to play with their mind,
taking a little rope and a very light pole,
telling them to stay put.

What the elephant doesn't realize yet is
that he can break loose of the hold
that man thinks he has on this huge creature.

Guess what, we are the same way.
Sometimes thinking like an elephant.
Not realizing that
we have the strength given to us by God
to conquer anything we set our minds to,
which is good according to Jesus's word.

It's time to take the rope
of limitation off our mind
and expand ourselves.

Learning to stop saying what we cannot do.

1 Peter 4:10-11

A Mother's Strength

As a single mother
trying to raise a son all alone,
I often wonder
if I could raise him to be strong,
with wonderful values
and respect for himself
and others around him.

I ask myself, did I teach him to have strength,
when the world wants to beat him down
for no reason,
knowing never to doubt himself?
And if he should fall,
he has the right to get back up
and try again?

Well, today I realize,
I was blessed with a mother's strength,
because when I look at my son
and see the man that he chose to become,
I must say, oh what a great job I have done.

But, I wasn't alone,
because I let God lead the way.

Proverbs 1:8-9

Behind Each Door

I took a peek behind door number one,
where I saw you standing there.

Now behind door number two,
I notice my heart had begun beating very fast.

I am at door number three,
I find myself telling me to slow down.

Now over to door number four I go.
I'm thinking,
let's be sure about all this,
but my heart wouldn't listen.

Here I am at the last door number five.
I see you standing there,
asking me to take your hand in marriage.

And if you all must know, I said,
Yes, I will.

1 Corinthians 7:36

Innocence

I gave my innocence away, trying to be loved
by any man who would love me back.
Please don't blame my mom
for what I am about to share with you,
because for a long time, she really didn't know
the hurt that I was feeling about my dad,
as he took away my chance
of being his little baby girl.

In front of my mother,
I was her little innocent girl.
But behind her back,
I was giving my innocence away
to any man that said I was pretty to him.
You see that's something my dad
never told me,
because he was blind when it came to me.

Now here I am,
learning what real love is all about,
after giving my innocence away.
Being loved by a wonderful Man
called Jesus Christ.

There is one thing that I did ask of the Lord,
and that is;
can I keep this little secret between Him and I,
because I don't want to cause my mother
any more hardship and pain.
And He said, "Yes"!

While wiping my tears away from my eyes,
God told me
that I will always be
His pretty little baby girl.

Ephesians 6:4

Suicidal Thinking

Doesn't always mean that someone wants to
physically kill themselves.

The Lord allows some of us to write,
so that we won't surrender
to our suicidal negative way of thinking,
because we can tear ourselves down
and feel like what's the use.

Our hunger pains
that our body sometimes feels,
while our minds play tricks on us.
Telling us, what does love have to do with it.

How quickly the Lord moves,
when He sees one of His own in deep trouble,
losing their way.

Calling out our names,
reminding us of a scripture or two.
Getting our mind renewed back on Him,
while giving us time to reconnect
with a new positive way of thinking.

Psalm 57:1

A Blessing

Recognizing a blessing sent by God,

with a pretty smile a loving heart,

Spreading love all over the place,

Unconditionally,

to everyone it meets.

Ezekiel 34:26

You Promise

Last night I felt God,

when He gave a part of my heart to you.

I heard you make a promise to Him,

that you will never misuse my heart
in any way.

And you also promise not to abuse it.

And you can believe,
that I am going to hold you to your word.

Hebrews 10:23

Used by Jesus in a Special Way

Wow!
Jesus used me in a special way.
Today there was this little old lady
that was bent over
standing by the stamp machine
looking at it as closely as she could,
trying to understand the little fine print.

As I was standing in line, I began noticing her.
Thinking to myself,
I wonder does she need some help,
I stepped out of line, walked over,
offering my help, asking her
what did she need.

She said, "baby,
sorry I can't look up to see you",
but I am trying to buy some stamps
out the machine".

"I'll look to see how much they cost", I told her.

She pulled out her money with no questions,
and she trusted me
to put her money in the stamp machine.

Then asking me to put everything back
in her purse saying,
"thank you baby very much".

I had to say, "no problem and thank you too".

She said, "for what, what did I do"?

I said, "you allowed God to use me
in a special way today.

So I thank you too".

1 Thessalonians 5:18

A Rare Opportunity

It's a rare opportunity
that we get a chance to meet
a guardian angel face to face.
Well, I was blessed to meet one.

She had golden red hair
with sparkling brown eyes.

A unique personality she had.
She even spoke in a very low voice,
offering me some H_2O.

She reached out to help me with all my bags
that I was struggling with.
Oh, I almost forgot,
she shared an apricot or two.

We both had so much fun
meeting as strangers,
but laughing like we knew each other
for a very long time.

I opened my poetry tablet,
that I write most of my poems in
from time to time.
She read a few.
Sharing with me how beautiful
she thought mine were.

Thank You Mrs. Mary Jo,
you are a guardian angel,
sent by God above.

Galatians 6:10

Cure for Loneliness

Knock Knock.
Who's there.
It's loneliness
back at my front door
trying to attack me in my home.

Once again, fighting the battle
of my life right now
because I can't go down in defeat.

Sorry, but loneliness
can't come in here anymore.

I guess I need to come up with an idea
to keep it out of here.

Please allow me to think for a second or two.

I got up and started opening
doors and windows
allowing the sound of life back in.

Just that fast,
I saw that attack of loneliness
run out the back door.

Psalm 31:1-5

Accepting

While you're speaking to me,
I will listen.

When you hug me,
I will accept it.

As you reach out to kiss me,
I will not fight it.

Baby, the more you are around me,
the more you will want to love me.

Romans 15:7

Surprise

Here we both are,
beginning to make wonderful history together.

Something we both
will be able to look back on,
as we begin moving forward.

Laughing at each other's silly jokes.

That special touch,
full of compassion between us.

But then, to my surprise,
as I began to get comfortable and exhale...

You decide to throw the towel in
and walk away marrying someone else.

Exodus 23:8

A Friendship Chosen by Heaven

One summer day,
I heard a knock at my front door.

I couldn't believe my eyes,
but there was an angel standing there.

From that day on,
neither one of us can explain
how quickly a friendship
chosen by heaven was in the making.

It seems like our meeting wasn't the first time,
because it was full of encouraging words
and plenty of laughter.

Thank You Lord,
for a friendship chosen by heaven.

Galatians 5:14

The Lucky One

Mirror, Mirror, on the wall,
today I am the luckiest of them all.

Because God used,
His own hands,
to create and mold me,
together in the image of Him.

Laughing to Himself,
He said job well done.
Then He took His breath and blew life in me,
that only He can give.

He has taken a person like me,
under His wings to teach and show me,
all that I can become in Him.

How much luck can one person have?

Genesis 1:27

God's Unchanging Hands

I am at a crossroad in my Christian walk.
Knowing already that I should go right,
instead of going wrong,
in making a heart to heart decision.

Fighting with everything I have learned.
All my Bible verses, church notes,
even the renewing of my mind.

Wow!

It only took a moment
for me to look away from God,
before I allowed myself to get caught up
with the way of the world.

A little lustful thinking
on my part with another Christian.

Willing to play the victim of the other party.

Just for a moment I thought it would be okay
to sneak into darkness
and play around for a while.

Thinking to myself,
this would be a little secret
between the both of us.

God, being who He is,
tapped me on the shoulder saying;
no, no My child, sorry but
you can't hide from Me.

I am the Most High.
Come unto Me My child,
and I will give you rest.

Don't fall for a temporary fix
of that lustful kiss that is full of deceit.
My child, you are better than that.
You are full of great things to come.

I am God Almighty,
and even I must take a stand back,
just so I can see,
just how much you truly do love Me.

I left you with a choice to do right or wrong.
That's your decision to make.
Oh, what an experience it was.
But now I must allow myself to exhale,
release the world back out.
Allowing my mind to be renewed
as I begin thanking the Lord
for keeping His unchanging hands upon me.

Matthew 11:28–30

To a Son of a Poetess

My son, as I have said so many times before,
I know without a shadow of a doubt,
that you were born full of possibilities,
and great things to come.

Please don't get discouraged along the way
because your sister and I are counting on you
to continue on against all odds.

Continue down the yellow brick road
that God has put there for you
so you don't lose your way.

Keep your eyes on the Most High.
Keep your heart warm toward others.
Keep your hands safe.

Because when the right time comes,
that is where the Lord
is going to bless you with strength
to hold onto what is to come.

This I write to you,
a son of a poet.

Ephesians 6:3

To a Daughter of a Poetess

Dear daughter of mine,
So many times I look your way,
thanking God each and every day,
for blessing me
with a wonderful daughter like you.

When I notice your laughter,
the tears in your eyes.
When I hear you sharing kind words to others,
lending someone a helping hand.

At night you take a few moments
to listen to your own daughter
as she says her prayers,
then you kiss her on her forehead,
tucking her in between the sheets.
The same way I used to do you
and your brother.

Baby girl, when I look at you,
my heart is filled with joy as I thank God
for blessing me with grace and mercy,
to raise you to be all that you can be.

I thank Him for keeping His hands upon me,
through the good and not so good times,
that sometimes came between us.

But one thing for sure, today,
when I look at you,
my dear daughter,
I can see a silhouette of me in you.

Ephesians 6:3

Pride

With my pride,
I moved out of a place I was calling home.
Selling all my belongings.
Yes, everything that I owned.

Sleeping on other people's sofas and chairs.
Feeling a little lost for a while.
Not caring anymore,
about my tomorrows.

One day Jesus stopped by,
asking me how was I feeling.
Then He said, dear child,
it's time for you to go back
where you left from your home.

But it's your decision to make.
Are you going to allow pride to block your way,
causing you to miss your blessings
of what is to come?

I began thinking quietly to myself.
The next thing I knew,
my heart started feeling warm again.

I leaped out on faith,,
packing my few things up,
making sure I thanked everyone
for their hospitality.

Returning back to the place
I once called home,
with nothing but my little sack of pride
that made me leave in the first place.

Having to sleep on the floor for a while,
showing the Lord that
He can trust me with a little,
and I will not complain anymore.

In a three bedroom house,
I was blessed with a house full of furnishings,
just in case someone comes
and needs a place to lay their head.

Jesus even blessed me with a house alarm,
to warn me when Satan is near.
But the most important lesson
I have learned in all this is;

We shouldn't have pride in our lives,
when we are serving the Most High.

Daniel 4:13 & Proverbs 8:13

Awaken

It's time to clothe yourself with strength.
Please shake the dust off your feet.
It's time to move on.

Get those heavy chains
from around your neck.

As long as you live, you're going to have bills.

Stop stressing what will happen,
if you should die tomorrow.

Does it make any sense to kill yourself
from worrying and stressing.

Well, that is not of God.
Surrender it all unto Him.
He's waiting to free you from debt.

But, only if you learn how to trust Him.

Nature Walk

Pretty blue waters running down the stream.

Wild purple and yellow flowers all around me.

Green trees beginning to turn a little brown
as summer comes to an end.

Mountains full of so much history
that has not been told yet.

Baby blue skies.

Puffy white clouds.

Birds flying high,
going east before the cold weather arrives.

Look at how bright the moon is tonight,
while we are enjoying
our nighttime nature walk.

Psalm 19:1-6

Rebuke Him

Life can throw things unexpectedly our way,
and it only happens most of the time,
when we want to help someone.

There Satan is,
trying to bring some hard knocks our way.

What Satan forgets is that
we have the right at any given time
to rebuke him.

Water My Soul

Water my soul
dear Lord,
while the rain is falling down.

Then no one will notice
the teardrops running down my face.

Caused by so many
disappointments and heartaches.

Matthew 11:29

Untitled

I know that the Lord speaks to me.
But for some strange reason,
I am getting it all wrong.

I feel as though I am a drifter.

Not knowing where I belong.

Maybe it's because I find myself
still trying to fix everybody's problems,
instead of fixing my own.

Does it really come a time,
when it's time to settle down,
or is it that we look backward so much
that we can't move into the present?

Psalm 89:15

Welcome to Our Home

Please come in our home.
We want you to enjoy your visit with us,
sharing in our warmth,
laughter and happiness.

We want you to know
that you are always welcome.

The only thing we ask of you
is that you leave all your negativity
outside the front door.

Now if you can do that,
then take your shoes off at the door,
and come on in, feel at home.

Would you like something to drink?

Can we offer you something to eat?

Have a seat,
and let's all laugh and chat for a while.

You're Leaving Me Now Sweetheart

You and I talked each night long distance.
Sharing our day,
before tucking one another in,
saying sleep tight.

Making our plans together,
for all our tomorrows.

Saying it will always be you and I.

Oh, how we both started laughing.
Couldn't stop talking
about our good times
we shared together last night.

Sweetheart, I think you knew,
because being who you are,
you was trying in your own special way,
to tell me,
and get me prepared for what was to come.

WOW!

High school sweethearts we were,
being blessed already by God
with a beautiful marriage,
full of wonderful memories for us to cherish.

I know now I must let you go, Baby.
So go 'head sweetheart, it's okay,
because Jesus already prepared
my heart last night,
for what was to come.

It's your time to accept your angel wings,
and you must put them on.

The other angels in heaven,
are having a celebration in your honor.

God did promise me that you will be okay.
I want you to remember
that I will always love you
with all my heart,
but God has the last say.

And no one can love us more than Him.

And that's God above all and everything.

Amen.

Attending School the Hard Way

The places we go to learn our life's lesson.

Some go to the jailhouses
while others go to the streets of hell.

Making bad choices.

Allowing pride to fill our heads.

Yes, I must ask you this.
what happens then

?

I Heard the Ant Scheme

I was sitting on my balcony
one summer afternoon thinking to myself
rather to get my ant spray
while looking at them crawl all over the place.

Well, I decided to leave them alone.

I said to myself,
hey, they are outside and
they are not bothering me.

As I continued to sit there,
I began to hear their scheme,
working hard together as a team,
doing the work for their queen.

Looking at them,
not one trying to hold the other one back.

When they see the other one coming
they step aside so the other one can pass.

Here I am learning something today
from a tiny little ant in size,
thinking how great God's kingdom would be
if we could learn to work together
just like them.

Isaiah 66:2

Angel Wings

Last night I took a look toward heaven's doors.
I could see my name
in the Lamb's Book of Life.

I've been praying for a while now,
asking God to do something
about the pain I was in.

Last night Jesus visited me
in my hospital room.

I told Him that I was tired of fighting
and taking all these medicines.

He granted me my wish, but I remember
that I had something special that I must do.

I began asking the Lord
to forgive me of all my sins.

He just laughed to Himself saying,
"my dear child I already know
your heart and it's okay".

Oh what a wonderful feeling that was.

Now it was time for me to take a deep breath,
as my eyes began to close.

Just that fast I was at peace,
knowing that I was home in heaven with Him.

To Our New Bundle of Joy

We can't find the words to express ourselves
about your arrival

Baby Name Here

As you grow from day to day
we will learn how to love you in a special way.

We gave God our word
that we would do right in raising you.

With plenty of love, caring, teaching
and showing you, our bundle of joy,
right from wrong.

As we take this new journey together
many mistakes will be made
on our part as new parents to you.

But we promise you
that everything in the long run
will turn out okay.

Daddy's Name_____

Mommy's Name_____

Date_____

Behind the Shadow of My Dreams

I know where I am right now.

It gets a little scary sometimes
because I don't know what will happen next.

So I find myself hiding
behind the shadows of my dreams.

Help Me Mother

Baby, I wish I could,
but as you can see right now,
I can't even help myself.

It took all these years for me to realize
that it wasn't my job
to become your best friend.

What I was supposed to do was
to raise you to fear God,
making Him the head of your life.

Learning to always love God unconditionally,
no matter what state you find yourself in.

Now you are calling me and all I know to do
is stand here confused
just when you need me the most.

What do I suppose to say to you?

Oh, what a joke I've been as your parent.
Look at you my child,
trying to stand there and defend yourself
when I haven't given you anything
to fight with.

Here I thought I had it going on.
Running the streets,
and running to the jail house,
taking care of some other mother's son.

Now that my son needs me,
who do I suppose to call on?

Please don't say,
Jesus Christ,
because He is not going to hear or respond
to a person like me.

All of a sudden I fell to my knees begging,
asking God to forgive me of all my sins.

Then I ask Him, dear Lord,
why did you forget about me?
All He said was, my child,
I didn't forget about you,
you ran away from me.

Lord I'm tired, I have been in so many places
that was not pleasing to you.
He said, "I know my child,
I was right there with you".

Father, I sold my soul just for a treat.
Showing my feet
to every guy that I would meet.

Dear Lord, my son is calling out to me,
what do I do?
Now here I am crying out to You
for the both of us.

Lord, please help me to help our dear son
Please!
In Jesus name,
Amen.

To Our Elders

May God continue to bless each one of you.
We thank you for your endurance,
going through so much
to make life a little easier
for generations to come.

So today, we salute you,
our elders for going over and
beyond your call of duty.

Leviticus 19:32

Mate

I often think about people,
and what they say to me.

I shared with them that
I sometime get a little lonely,
and mention I would love to have a mate.

Most women who are going through something
will say, girl, you don't know,
it's better to be by yourself.

My question to them is,
if it's so good being by myself,
then you need to plead your case;

Because the other day
when you were praying out loud,
I heard you praying to the Lord,
for Him to send you a mate,
or either save your marriage.

Please tell me, what's up with that?
Oh it's good enough for you to have one
but it's not okay for me to have a mate?

Thank God I don't always listen
to what other people have to say.

Free

This morning I thought, just for today,
I will take public transportation
instead of riding in my car all day.

What a wonderful idea it turned out to be.
A whole new experience it was.
I was seeing things
that I never get a chance to see.

Never paying attention to all of God's creation
that is all around me.
Even nice people riding on the bus,
going to work, school and
wherever else they are going.

Others are eager to put a smile on your face.
Sharing a kind word or two,
while the bus driver is making sure
that everyone is getting
where they are going safe.
That beats riding in a car all day.

Free exercise.
Having to walk fast doing a little running
to catch the next bus.
WOW!
I am getting a chance to exercise
free for a day.
Maybe, if it doesn't rain tomorrow,
I will catch the bus and not ride in the car.
Then I can get some more
free smiles, hellos and exercise.
It will be nice if you would
join in with me today

A True and Wonderful Friend

People often look past
a true and wonderful friendship.

When I called your name out for the first time,
with no questions asked,
you stepped in as a best friend would do.

You are a friend
that only a few people will meet in a lifetime.

Please always remember,
having a friend like you is always knowing
I have a best friend indeed.

Dancing in the Rain

Last night Jesus and I were
dancing in the rain,
but I could only see two footprints.

I asked why was that and He answered,
"this is how it is when you ask for forgiveness
of your sins".

I always make sure that I
wash your past sins away,
so that no one will be able to recognize
what my child has been through.

Little Blue Bird

You have been putting up a good fight
for years,
playing hide and go seek with me.

You forgot that I can see everything you do.
Did you forget that too?

Well little blue bird,
that's how I knew how to find you
when you got a little confused
and turned around.

You were out of it for a little while
but as always,
I had a few guardian angels
watching over you.

I'm more than sure
you didn't recognize any of them,
but the first ones were
the people that passed by
and saw you lying there in your car
over the steering wheel and they called 911.

The second angel was the police.
Yes, I have a few of them working for me too.

And last, but not least,
was all the wonderful doctors
and nurses that was waiting for your arrival.

Yes, I was right there
making sure that everything was going okay,
little blue bird, for you.

One Day

I would like to meet Jesus Christ
one day as I listen to Him saying,

My sister, the task that the Father and I
trusted you with,
We both would like to say to you,
job well done.

And for that reason
the both of Us would love to meet you also,
one day.

I Lost

Offensiveness
Negativity
Enemies

Hatred
Unfaithfulness
Naughtiness
Dismay
Rejection
Envy
Discouragement

Pride
Overindulgence
Uncleanness
Neediness
Disobedience
Sinful Thinking

By the Grace of God

Park Residence

When I go to the park
for my morning jog,
I share a few teardrops there.

I don't worry about anything,
because only heaven can see them.

The grass soaks each one of them up,
not leaving a trace that I've been there,
releasing all the doubt, hurt and shame,
and the ugliness
I feel inside my soul.

I try very hard to hurry up
and renew my thoughts because I know
it's an attack from satan,
trying to rob, steal and destroy my happiness.

So I can't give up, feeling defeated,
because I am a child of God.

Leave Them There

My child is out of control again
and I don't know what to do anymore.

As I was walking past this lady and her child,
I heard in her voice
that she was at her wit's end.

I just had to say, "excuse me miss,
I understand what you are going through.
I am a mother too".

May I share a few things with you
or maybe I should have said,
can I ask you a question or two?

When you was carrying your child,
that is standing here, in your womb,
did you nourish them,
by talking and praying to them?

When they were born,
did you get your children and yourself dressed,
so all of you could go
and attend Sunday school
when they was the age of 0-10?

At night before tucking them in bed,
did you take time,
as tired as you may have been,
did you take time to teach them their prayers?

Then when they became this
rebellious pre-teen and so on,
and no matter what they had to say,
you made them go to church anyway.

Well let me share this with you
from one mother to another mother,
this may sound a little cold hearted to you...

It's time to give God back His child,
and this time leave them there.

Laughter

When I am in the presence of others,
the conversation is always about me.

From the time we gather around,
all their so-called funny
and negative jokes is always toward me.

Then they get upset
when I don't care to join in their laughter.

For what, when it's about me?

I don't care to laugh
about something negative
being said about me.

A Flowing Angel

I am a flowing angel,
I go where God sends me
and needs me the most,
as long as I carry life in me.

I have no permanent place
to be here on earth.

Peace be still is what the sweet song says.

You may sing that song to me,
when I have laid down for the last time
on my everlasting bed.

Now in the meantime,
I must continue on my way.

Telling people everywhere I go
about the book that was written
in Jesus's name.

Now you know just who I am.

The flowing angel
that Jesus has sent ahead.

Words of Encouragements to Others
Who Also Suffer From Fear and Doubt

There are so many people in the world who are blessed just like me with a natural talent that God has blessed them with. But for whatever reason, and believe me we have a lot of excuses why we don't do what God has created for us to do. Maybe for the same reason I wasn't doing it and that is because I didn't know that I had the gift. When God revealed it to me I started coming up with so many excuses until I couldn't think of any more. Then I start comparing myself to others and everything else.

What I would like to do is; each time the Lord blesses me with another wonderful book of poetry I would like to call someone out that I know personally to take a stand and come forth against all odds and begin believing in themselves and doing what it takes to get their dream (gift) started.

I think when God blesses someone to do something out of the ordinary it's a reason and I think this is what He is using me for. He wants me to show so many others that when He gives us something to do He will equip us with what we need rather its people or material things. I have truly been blessed with meeting wonderful people around me to get the job done and it's helping with my shyness.

To all my other readers, who knows, the next time it might be you! E-mail me your dreams and I promise I will pray about it and stand in agreement with you. We must first learn to believe and love ourselves before we can make anyone else believe in our dreams. Still today, I have to work on that myself each and every day.

a

Dear Lord;

Thank You for keeping your arms around me protecting me from all hurt, harm and danger while I was working hard day and night letting my best come forth in completing this wonderful book.

Now Lord the book is done. I am praying that it will go where it needs to go, helping people to believe. no matter what circumstances they find themselves in, they will grow by learning to pick up and dust their Bibles off and begin growing and understanding Your Word. Knowing that You are God all by Yourself

And then Lord from time to time they can steal away and read:
"The Covering Of God"

Or our first book

"Inspirational Words Of The Heart"

Inspired By: *The Holy Spirit*

Penned by:
Rev. Lennell Haley, KIRM INC Ministries

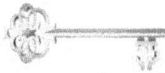

It's time for you to use the key "the measure of faith" to unlock your gifts that your Heavenly Father has given you, because you can do all things through Jesus Christ who strengthens you

Philippians 4:13

b

ACKNOWLDGEDMENTS & SPECIAL THANKS

I would like to give a special thank you to my supportive editor, Deidra Tutt Jackson, Jade Business Resources, Sherrie Wallace; and C. King Photography, Luray, VA who blessed me with the photography cover wrap for this book..

To the family God has blessed me with; my son, Charell and my daughter, Jonell.

To my beautiful grandchildren Jazmine, Mateo and Brennell.

To my parents and namesake; Jonell Wright Kirby, my wonderful mother and my dad, LeRoy Haley, Sr. and my step-dad; Kirby.

To my siblings; brothers LeRoy (Jr) and Darryl, Nathaniel and Ebed and my sisters; Shariel and Sandra.

Thank you to two very thoughtful people who goes by the name of Orlando and Shirlen Debose from Tulsa, Oklahoma.

And last but not least; thank you to all who bought my first book. *"Inspirational Words Of The Heart"* and who bought this book, *The Covering of God.*

Thank You Jesus for preparing me for this moment.

Just A Thought

You too can join ME under
"The Covering Of God"

We put no stumbling block in anyone's path
so that our ministry will not be discredited.
Rather, as servants of God,
we commend ourselves in every way;
in great endurance,
in troubles, hardships and distresses,
in beatings, imprisonments and riots,
in hard work, sleepless nights, and hunger,
in purity, understanding, patience, and
kindness,
in the Holy Spirit, and in sincere love,
in truthful speech, and in the power of God,
with weapons of righteousness
in the right hand
and in the left,
through glory and dishonor,
bad report and good report,
genuine, yet regarded as impostors,
known, yet we live on,
beaten and yet not killed,
sorrowful, yet always rejoicing,
poor, yet making many right,
having nothing,
and yet possessing everything.

2 Corinthians 6:3-10

d

AUTHOR'S MESSAGE:

First, giving God, all the praise and glory. I thank Him one more time for blessing me with His mercy and grace. I would like to say thank you, everyone, for sharing your kind words and supporting me by buying my first book, *"Inspirational Words of the Heart."*

I truly thank each and every one of you from the bottom of my heart.

With all my imperfections, I'm still growing and learning how to become all that God wants me to be, understanding that one day I will be perfect in Him. I am enjoying myself with all the opportunities I'm receiving from the Lord, through meeting so many wonderful people from all walks of life.

Oh, what a blessing this has been, knowing that my writing is truly a blessing from the Holy Spirit. If He doesn't give it to me, I have nothing to write because I didn't go to school to learn to write and I have no special training. I have been blessed with the spirit of discernment. The Holy Spirit whispers in my ear, and I pick up a piece of paper and pen and began writing down the words I hear. So, I know without a doubt that my poetry comes by the way of what non-Christians believe is the unknown. But I am a Christian, and I know that there is a God above who has equipped us to do the impossible through Him, with no worldly explanations, knowing by faith that any and everything is done through Him, my Lord and Savior, Jesus Christ.
Amen.

e